797,885 Books

are available to read at

Forgotten Books

www.ForgottenBooks.com

Forgotten Books' App
Available for mobile, tablet & eReader

ISBN 978-1-330-70389-2
PIBN 10094609

This book is a reproduction of an important historical work. Forgotten Books uses state-of-the-art technology to digitally reconstruct the work, preserving the original format whilst repairing imperfections present in the aged copy. In rare cases, an imperfection in the original, such as a blemish or missing page, may be replicated in our edition. We do, however, repair the vast majority of imperfections successfully; any imperfections that remain are intentionally left to preserve the state of such historical works.

Forgotten Books is a registered trademark of FB &c Ltd.
Copyright © 2015 FB &c Ltd.
FB &c Ltd, Dalton House, 60 Windsor Avenue, London, SW19 2RR.
Company number 08720141. Registered in England and Wales.

For support please visit www.forgottenbooks.com

1 MONTH OF FREE READING

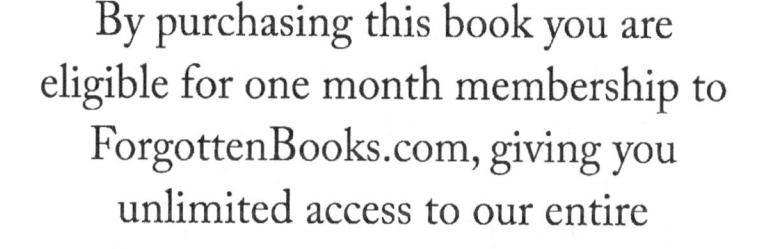

at

www.ForgottenBooks.com

By purchasing this book you are eligible for one month membership to ForgottenBooks.com, giving you unlimited access to our entire collection of over 700,000 titles via our web site and mobile apps.

To claim your free month visit: www.forgottenbooks.com/free94609

* Offer is valid for 45 days from date of purchase. Terms and conditions apply.

English
Français
Deutsche
Italiano
Español
Português

www.forgottenbooks.com

Mythology Photography **Fiction**
Fishing Christianity **Art** Cooking
Essays Buddhism Freemasonry
Medicine **Biology** Music **Ancient Egypt** Evolution Carpentry Physics
Dance Geology **Mathematics** Fitness
Shakespeare **Folklore** Yoga Marketing
Confidence Immortality Biographies
Poetry **Psychology** Witchcraft
Electronics Chemistry History **Law**
Accounting **Philosophy** Anthropology
Alchemy Drama Quantum Mechanics
Atheism Sexual Health **Ancient History**
Entrepreneurship Languages Sport
Paleontology Needlework Islam
Metaphysics Investment Archaeology
Parenting Statistics Criminology
Motivational

ANCIENT EARTH FORTS

OF THE

Cuyahoga Valley, Ohio,

BY

COL. CHAS. WHITTLESEY,

PRESIDENT OF THE WESTERN RESERVE AND NORTHERN OHIO
HISTORICAL SOCIETY.

PUBLISHED FOR THE SOCIETY BY A GENTLEMAN OF CLEVELAND.

CLEVELAND, OHIO:
FAIRBANKS, BENEDICT & CO., PRINTERS.
1871.

ANCIENT EARTH FORTS

OF THE

Cuyahoga Valley, Ohio,

BY

COL. CHAS. WHITTLESEY,

PRESIDENT OF THE WESTERN RESERVE AND NORTHERN OHIO HISTORICAL SOCIETY.

PUBLISHED FOR THE SOCIETY BY A GENTLEMAN OF CLEVELAND.

CLEVELAND, OHIO:
FAIRBANKS, BENEDICT & CO., PRINTERS.
1871.

Jar
E14
O3W6

2111

Ancient Earth Works of Ohio.

HISTORY OF THE SURVEYS.

The existence of ancient earth works in Ohio was first brought to notice by the Rev. David Jones, in 1772-3; by Arthur Lee, in 1784; and in 1785, through a plan and description of those at Marietta, by Capt. JONATHAN HEART, of Colonel Harmar's battalion.

Capt. Heart assisted in building Fort Harmar, at the mouth of the Muskingum river. He was evidently a man of education, and had served in the Revolutionary army. His survey was made while the ground was yet covered with a heavy growth of forest trees.

In 1801, the Rev. Mr. Harris, while on a tour through the Ohio country, resurveyed them and inserted an engraved plan in his published Journal.

Caleb Atwater, Esq., of Circleville, Ohio, made the first general survey of the Ohio Earth Works in 1819, under the auspices and at the expense of the American Archæological Society, at Worcester, Mass.

His plans and descriptions fill an important portion of the first volume of their transactions, published in 1820. When the first Geological Survey of Ohio was in progress, I continued the survey of the newly discovered works, intending to make the subject of our antiquities a part of the final report.

This survey came to an end in 1839, without a final report. J. H. SULLIVANT, Esq., of Columbus, requested me to continue this part of the survey at his expense, with a view to publication by himself.

My plans included all the ancient works then known, but Mr. Sullivant's health failing, they were not published, and many of them were lost.

In 1845, the Hon. E. George Squier, who has since done so much to develop the Archæology of the United States, commenced a resurvey of them in connection with Dr. E. H. Davis, both of Chillicothe, Ohio.

These gentlemen made the first systematic descriptions with figures, of the numerous relics of the Mound Builders. They operated under the auspices of the Smithsonian Institute at Washington. The results of their labors, fully illustrated, constitute the first volume of its Contributions.

Their surveys in this State were confined to the works on waters of the Ohio. A part of my plans were published with theirs, and a part in May, 1850, as Article 7, Vol. 3, of the Contributions, which relate principally to the works on the waters of Lake Erie.

Ancient Inhabitants

OF THE

MISSISSIPPI VALLEY AND THE LAKE REGIONS.

Ruins of ancient earth works are plainly to be seen throughout a large part of the United States, constructed by a people who preceded the race first encountered here by the whites. These works are numerous on the Ohio river and on the streams which discharge into it. They are also found, but of a quite different character, on the streams which empty into Lakes Erie and Ontario from the South. Here, all or nearly all of them have a military purpose, and are less imposing than those on the waters of the Ohio.

In Wisconsin is another and quite a different type of ancient earth works, which are principally mounds, in the form of effigies of animals.

It does not follow that the builders of these different styles of works were one nation or were cotemporary. They had, however, traits enough in common to be ranked as a *race*, under the denomination of *" Earth Builders."* These differences were also sufficiently marked to require a separation into nations or tribes; occupying territories easily defined. The people who inhabited Central and Southern Ohio, also covered an extensive country farther to the southward and westward; down the great valley of the Mississippi to the Gulf of Mexico. They are already known by the name of *" Mound Builders."*

To distinguish the three peoples by their most marked characters, I designate those on the Ohio as the *Agricultural nation;* the Fort Builders on the lakes as the *Military nation,* and those between the Mississippi and Lake Michigan as the *Effigy nation*. Those who wish to study the works of the "Mound Builders" are referred to the elaborate descriptions of Messrs. Squier and Davis. The remains of the "Fort Builders" in New York have been surveyed and described by Mr. Squier, in the year 1849. The Effigy mounds of Wisconsin were surveyed by Dr. I. A. Lapham, of Milwaukee. The results of his work are to be found in the Contributions for 1855.

From the water-shed of the rivers that discharge southerly into the Ohio and the Mississippi, near the 40th parallel of north latitude, southerly to the Gulf of Mexico, including Arkansas and Texas, there is a similarity in the style of the ancient works, indicating that they are the work of one people.

Their leading pursuit was agriculture, having little use for military defences. Their most striking works are burial mounds of earth or loose stone, and altar pyramids, showing a large religious development.

In the effigy region, west of Lake Michigan, it is less easy to devine the leading characteristics of their builders. In the third division of this ancient population, occupying the lake country, in Ohio and New York, military defences take the lead, but their works are far less prominent.

There are certain things which all these people had in common, though they possessed very different degrees of advancement. They all erected earth monuments over the remains of some of their dead, while the bodies of the many were consumed by fire. They had native copper as their only metal, obtained from the mines of Lake Superior, which were extensively wrought

All of them used implements of flint and other stones in a great variety of forms, which are similar, though not identical with those of the red man of our times. Their copper tools, spear heads, spades and knives, were numerous and superior in form and finish to the few and rude copper knives of Indians, which were made from stray nuggets, found in the glacial drift.

It would seem that their dwellings and their weapons of war were principally of wood; but we are as yet in comparative ignorance in regard to both.

Comparison of the Pre-Historic Races

IN EUROPE AND AMERICA.

EUROPE.

PRIMITIVE MAN.

Cave dwellers cotemporary with the elephant, mastodon, rhinoceros, cave bear, cave lion, cave hyena, and the great stag, all now extinct; and with the closing out of the glacial or drift era, there known as diluvium—they were hunters, dressed in skins—had stone and flint implements, without polish—and pottery. Antiquity exceeding fifteen thousand years.

SECOND ERA.

Polished implements of stone and flint; domestic animals, with pottery, but no pipes, no tools of metal—not cultivators of the soil—hunters with the bow and spear—dress in skins.

AMERICA.

PRIMITIVE MAN.

In South and Central America cotemporary with the elephant, mastodon and extinct horse, dwellers in caves. In North America, evidence, though not as yet conclusive, to show him here as early as the diluvium or later drift; with the elephant, mastodon, extinct horse and megalonyx. Implements, dress and antiquity not known.

SECOND ERA.

In the Mississippi Valley copper cutting tools, beads, daggers, spears, ornaments and spades—cultivated the soil—built earth forts and mounds: polished stone axes and implements, rare. No beasts of burden—flint knives, arrow heads and other implements and weapons of stone, rare; stone calls or whistles and spindle whorls; beads made of bone and shells—domicils not known—had burial mounds for the dead—pipes of stone and clay—coarse cloth of hemp or nettles—miners of copper—cotemporary with the beaver and bear. Antiquity four to five thousand years. Slight evidence of an intervening race between the mound builder and the primitive man.

AGE OF BRONZE.
THIRD ERA.

Lake dwellings of wood; domestic animals; cultivate the soil; nets and cloth of flax; flint implements; cutting tools of bronze (alloy of copper and tin), with handles of bone and wood; pottery; dress in skins. Antiquity six thousand to seven thousand years; calls or whistles of bone; earth forts with ditches.

RED MEN AS THEY WERE BEFORE THE DISCOVERY OF AMERICA.

Hunters with spears and arrow heads; knives and daggers of flint, with stone mauls or axes; and flesh or skin scrapers—very little cultivation of the soil—mats and nets made of bark; a few and rude tools, gorgets and ornaments of copper; not workers of copper mines; not builders of earth forts with ditches; their forts made of wood and stones—dress in skins—no metal axes—no horses—domicils of bark and skins, or wooden frames covered with brush and earth—used rock shelters, and made inscriptions on trees, clay banks and rocks.

This comparison indicates on this continent quite a diversity from the old; in the progress of the early races towards civilization. Here the metal age preceded that of stone, corresponding better with the age of bronze, or of alloys in Europe. We have no certain representative of the rough or unpolished stone period, which there preceded the age of polished stone implements. Our "Mound Builders" were as far advanced, as their fabricators of bronze. From them there was a relapse towards a barbarism nearly entire, in their successors, the red Indian of the North. Of the diluvial man in America we know as yet almost nothing.

SURVEYS ON THE CUYAHOGA.

Since 1850 works have been reported that were not then known to me. Such of them as lie on or near the Cuyahoga river, I have since then, from time to time, examined, and now give a condensed description of them with illustrations. To make the subject complete, it is necessary to republish in this connection those heretofore described. In 1869, some of the members of the Western Reserve Historical and Archæological Society, located at Cleveland, gave me their assistance on those surveys and excavations, particularly, Dr. J. H. Salisbury, Vice-President; Dr. E. Sterling and C. C. Baldwin, Esq.

About this time the Society was enabled, through the liberality of a gentleman of Cleveland, to make more extended and systematic researches, and to publish the results.

It is possible that all the old earth works of this valley are not yet discovered. They are even in an undisturbed condition, not very prominent, the embankments seldom exceeding three feet in height, with a ditch of equal depth. In old fields that have been under cultivation twenty-five to forty years, none but a practiced eye would detect them. Fifty years since this country was but little settled; most of it being then covered with a heavy forest. When the old forts were from time to time discovered they attracted little attention.

The soil within them is invariably rich, owing to prolonged occupation in ancient times by human beings. This fact the early settlers soon discovered, and for this reason these grounds have been cropped closer than those of poorer soil. The plow, the drag, and the cultivator, have thus done extra work in leveling the parapets and filling the ditches of fort builders.

The earth works of the Cuyahoga are a fair representative of the military nation, extending from the west end of Lake Erie, north-eastwardly along the southern shore of Lake Ontario and the river St. Lawrence to Lake Champlain. There are very few on the immediate bank of the lakes. None are reported north of the lakes. They were built on bluffs and bends of the rivers, in strong defensive positions, near springs and small streams of water, not far from batteau navigation, and in the vicinity of rich bottom lands.

The territory of this people in Ohio may be seen by reference to the miniature outline map of the State, presented on Plate III. Those represented by a circular blot, belong to them. Those represented by a square or rectangle, are works of the "Mound Builders." Between them is a wide space of neutral or unoccupied country, on the head waters of the streams which flow in opposite directions, through the State. In this space there are no earth forts, or they have not yet fallen under my observation. I shall refer hereafter to the differences between these ancient nations, as shown in their implements and their works, the only records of their pursuits and their character, which are accessible to us.

Fort No. 1—Newburg.

The topographical surroundings of this fort are seen at once on the engraving, Plate II. It occupies one of the numerous headlands that project from a gravelly plain towards the rivulets which have, in the progress of ages, excavated these deep and nearly impassible ravines. The sides of the adjacent gullies are as steep as the earth will lie, and are wet and slippery from springs. Probably there was some defence of pickets or brush in the form of abattis, around the crest of the space within the double wall. Through the outer one, no gateway or open passage was left. This is not uncommon in the old earth forts. There must have been some mode of entering them, over the walls by stairs or ladders that could easily be removed.

Like most of those on the Cuyahoga and on the waters of Lake Erie, this was evidently a fortified village; like those of the Colorado Indians, in New Mexico, and the strong holds of the ancient Canaanites in Palestine, into which the inhabitants entered at night. The banks are now from one and a half to two feet above the natural surface, and the ditches two feet below. About one-fourth of a mile south-east, on the same level plain, is a mound which was ten feet high in 1847, but has since been much reduced by the plow.

Fort No. 2—Newburg.

This is smaller in size than any of those which stud the river bluffs. It is simply a projecting point, rendered more defensible by a bank of earth and a moat. The view from it is quite commanding and picturesque. Its position is about midway between Nos. 1 and 3, about one and a half miles below Lock No. 8, on the right bank of the river. At the middle, the ditch was never excavated, but there is no opening in the wall at this point. There is a narrow passage around the south end of the embankment along the edge of the ravine, by which the work may be entered. The soil is dry and sandy. In 1850 it had not been long in cultivation, and the elevation of the wall above the bottom of the ditch varied from four to six feet.

Fort No. 3—Independence.

There is little difference between this and No. 1, except in size. The interior wall is now wholly obliterated—the outer one with its ditch nearly so. A resurvey in 1870 disclosed a slight bank at $a\,a$, parallel with the bluff, for which there is no apparent object, nor for the horse-shoe outwork, $c\,c$.

As the soil within the lines is very rich it has been mercilessly cropped during one generation, and is still not exhausted. A rank growth of corn was waving over the entire enclosure in August last. About one-fourth of a mile southerly along the bluff, Mr. Henry Tuttle, the owner of the land, has found numerous relics and bones of the Indian race, indicating the site of a village. Among them is a small neatly carved pipe from the famous red pipe-stone quarry on the Coteau de Missouri, in Dakota. It is in the form of the head of a bird, and is among the collections of the Society, donated by Mr. Chas. Tuttle.

Fort No. 4—South-east part of Independence—Plate II.

Mr. Dickson, whose daughter, Mrs. Roreback, still resides on the premises, cleared the enclosed space A, in the year 1810. The embankment, b, was then three or four feet high. A house and barn were built upon it, which are there now, and little can be seen of its primitive condition. It is not certain there was a ditch.

There are springs of perpetual flow in the river bluff and in the adjacent ravines. Within the space A, near the mound, great numbers of human bones have been plowed up, so many that they were collected and reburied. The position is beautiful and commanding. On the same farm now owned by Messrs. DAVID L. and N. A. PHILIPS, about half a mile east there are four small mounds, nearly levelled by long cultivation. Near the township corners, about one-third of a mile south of these, is another mound which was five feet high when the early settlers first saw it. Polished stone implements were once common in this vicinity. One presented by Mr. Philips is in the Society's Cabinet, which is different from anything hitherto described. It is a soft crystalline coarse grained sienite, cut into the form of an acorn, with a flat base and a groove around it. Its length is two and a half inches, and its base an inch and eight-tenths.

Fort No. 5 and Cachès—Plate III.

When this fort was surveyed in 1847, the ancient pits across the ravine on the east were not known. Mr. L. Austin, of this city, first apprised me of their existence and went with me to the spot. I cannot say that there is any connection or relation between them and the fort. There are similar pits but more regular and circular in and around the space A, which were regarded by the early settlers as wells, because most of them contained water.

The hard-pan of this level space, only a part of which is enclosed, is not favorable for cachè pits, but the appearance of those on the crest of the bluff is the same as at C. For a time I regarded them as the remains of pit dwellings, both at the fort and and at B, C. With the assistance of Messrs. A. B. and Lorin Bliss, of Northfield, I made trenches through some of those in the group B. No relics, ashes or charcoal was discovered in them, such as are invariably found in the ancient pit dwellings of England. My present conviction is that they are cachès, and the work of the red men. A further notice of them will be found below.

It is necessary to add little to the exhibit given in the plate in respect to this fort. The engineers who selected the site understood its natural advantages, but it is not apparent why they left a part of the plateau without their lines, or why the wall is single on that side and the ditch is within it.

The earth of the bluffs is as steep as it will stand, and the ravines as well as the river, furnish abundance of water. Before the ground was cultivated, a man standing in the ditches could not look over the embankment. Along the sharp ridge or "hogs back," *e e,* there is barely room for a single team to pass. On this side there was no gateway or entrance, but at the west end of the inner parapet, there was a very narrow passage around it. The main entrance was evidently from the river side, near where the present road ascends the hill. Inside the lines the ground was much richer than without them. The mounds are small, and have not been explored. Pieces of flint, pottery and wrought stone implements, are numerous in the space A. They are of the Indian type. The cachès at B C, are on a level with the fort, and the ravine between them is sixty and seventy feet deep. As their strongest apprehensions of attack were from the country side, it is not probable that the fortress would have its magazines so far away, more than fifty rods distant, in an exposed position, beyond a very difficult gulf. As the present red race have made similar pits for storing their corn, and wild rice, it is reasonable to attribute all works of that kind to them. But in no instance, have the northern tribes been known to have occupied earth forts at, the period when they were first known to the whites, and rarely if ever since. We must therefore regard the forts, as the work of a different and an older race.

Fort No. 6—Boston.

This work is situated on the land of WILLIAM and RANDOLPH ROBINSON, on an elevated point of the river bluffs, near the east bank of the Cuyahoga, and near the south line of the township. It is upon ground very inaccessible, elevated about one hundred feet above the river. Its general topography, extent and form are fully shown on Plate V. As the ground has not been cultivated, and is now covered with full-grown oaks, the work is as near its first condition, as is possible after the lapse of centuries. The walls are low—seldom more than a foot above the natural surface, and two to two and one-half feet above the bottom of the ditches, which are double. At *a* is an opening only a few feet wide, and at *b* a broader one of twenty-one feet.

Very likely the slides at C have carried down a part of the wall on that side. Outside the work, the unenclosed space A A, is on a level with the terreplein B. Why, in this and several other of the Cuyahoga forts, there should have been left around the parapets, a level place above the bluff, for the convenience of the assailants, can not easily be explained.

From the center of one ditch to the center of the other is ten to fourteen feet. C. C. Baldwin, Esq., of the Society, and the Messrs. Robinson assisted at the survey.

About a mile up the valley to the south, on the same or eastern bank, is a mound which has been much lowered by long cultivation. It is situated on NATHAN POINT's land, upon the second terrace, about fifty feet above the river, and one-fourth of a mile from it. The brothers O. K. and W. K. Brooks, of Cleveland, and Mr. Baldwin volunteered to employ what remained of the day in opening this mound. It was then three feet above the natural surface, which is a dry, sandy plain. At two and one-half feet below the natural surface, they found parts of two human skeletons, with charcoal and ashes, showing that they had been burned. Only a few and small portions of the skull were sound enough to be raised or handled, and these soon fell to pieces. Even the teeth were soft and rotten, except their enameled crowns.

With the remains were two flint arrow points, without notches at the base, one of which is represented on Plate VIII. There was also a small thumb and finger stone, such as are common on the surface along the valley, and a portion of a call or whistle, fabricated from a piece of iron ore. It is nearly the same in size and figure, with the one from a mound in Cleveland, as figured on the same plate.

Another and larger one was found on the surface in Northfield. The arrow points, thumb stones and whistles were evidently articles highly prized by, and therefore necessary to the parties buried there.

At first we supposed that this arrow head, without a neck, was typical of the Mound Builder, and would serve to separate those of the red men, from those of his predecessor. On this account it was accurately sketched by Mr. W. J. Rattle, and engraved for this pamphlet. But flint arrow points have since been found on the surface, without the usual notchings at the base; and which may have been wrought and used by the recent Indians.

On the plains it is reported that arrows provided with poison, for use in war, are not securely fastened to the shaft. They are intended to remain in the wound. Those designed for killing game are notched, and firmly tied in a slit at the end of the shaft.

Mr. Austin and other gentlemen of the Society have seen some relics procured in the southerly part of this township, on the west side of the river. They were found, in excavating a cellar, within a small circle or hexagon of earth, about thirty-five feet in diameter. Among them was a copper knife about twelve inches long, very perfect, a copper awl or bodkin, four or five inches in length, and a copper chisel. These tools evidently belonged to the Mound Builders. There were several stone implements, and large pieces of mica; also, a piece of galena or lead ore. Most of the stone implements are scattered and probably lost. One of them had a figure, not heretofore observed in this region. It was made of the fine-grained, striped, greenish gray metamorphic slate of Lake Superior, and highly polished. Its length is four inches, the cross section everywhere a circle in form, like a short rolling pin, with a bilge in the middle. The diameter at each end is about an inch, at the middle an inch and a half, tapering from the center to the ends in a curve, everywhere symmetrical. Dr. Sterling says the Indians of the Pacific Coast have similar stones, by means of which they play games of chance.

Fort No. 7—Plate V.

Across the valley from the mound which was opened, is the stronghold No. 7, on the west side of the river, in a south-west direction, about a mile and a half distant.

Its position and general characteristics can be readily ascertained from the sketch, and the notes attached to it. It is neither very extensive nor imposing. The plateau A is not strictly inaccessible, but may easily be defended. Not more than one mounted man, could ride at once along the narrow ridge *h h*, which connects this tongue of land with the country in the rear. About one hundred and fifty feet beyond this narrow pass, is a broad bank and ditch, extending partly across the space between the bluffs. It has passages at the ends forty-four and twenty-one feet wide. The pits *c c* have precisely the aspect of modern cachès of the northern Indians, and were doubtless made by them.

It is less than half a mile in a south-west direction to the enclosed cachès represented on Plate VII. The village of Niles is about half a mile to the north. In this vicinity, in the townships of North Hampton and Bath, is a numerous group of mounds, cachès and embankments, which are shown on the map, Plate I.

Earthwork No. 8, Plate VI, belongs to this cluster of ancient remains. It is a low bank, without a ditch, situated near the river, on the second terrace, which is about thirty feet above the channel.

In the rear, and overlooking it, is higher land in the form of a terrace, and drift knolls. This is on the land of Mr. RICHARD HOWE, between the road and the river. Near the house of Mr. P. W. OSBORNE, adjoining it on the north, on the ridge, *b*, is a mound which is now four and one-half feet high, after being plowed over many years. Across the road to the north-west, half a mile distant, is another, in which a human skull was found seventeen years ago, reputed to be that of a Mound Builder.

With the assistance of Mr. Andrew Hale and his son, we made an open cut through this mound, without discovering anything but a few human bones near the top, evidently a burial much more recent than the erection of the mound; a stone chisel and a flint arrow point. It is composed of rich surface soil of a dark color. Originally it was seven feet high, now five feet, one diameter being forty-nine and the other forty-seven and one-half feet. Mr. Waggoner saw the skull plowed out of the mound, and is satisfied it lay near the surface. It is evidently more modern than the Mound Builders.

Between this mound and the cachès on Hale's Brook, Plate VII, are six small mounds, which Mr. Osborne and others have opened at different times, and in which are human bones and charcoal.

EARTHWORKS NOS. 8 AND 10—PLATE VI.

No. 8 is a low bank of earth, generally less than a foot in height, with an average breadth at base of nine feet. It has no ditch, and its situation precludes the idea of a design for a fort. The ground is yet a forest of venerable oaks, one of which stands on the embankment in full vigor, having a diameter of three feet.

If we had proof that the Indians or the Mound Builders had domestic animals, this work and the one in Granger, (No. 10,) not represented among the plates, might be taken for permanent corrals, surrounded with pickets as a protection against wild animals.

No. 10 is nearly a circle, eighteen rods in diameter, with a wall two feet high (1850) and ten feet broad, having one opening. The ditch is about equal in dimensions to the bank. It is situated upon ground lower than the general level of the country, except on the north-west, where there is a large swamp. Near it on the west is a terrace several feet higher. On each side are two small rivulets of permanent water. The road running east from the center, passes through it at about half a mile, but the owner had, twenty years since, nearly leveled it with the natural surface, for the accommodation of his house, barn and outhouses.

FORT NO. 9—PLATE VI.

This work is situated on a high and very precipitous bluff, on the land of JOHN HOVEY. He has been laboring during many years to obliterate it, by turning the furrows always towards the ditch, which has now nearly disappeared. Originally the bank was more bold than is usual in the Cuyahoga forts, being full six feet above the bottom of the moat.

In its general characters and position it resembles No. 6, on Robinson's land, in Boston. In both of them only a part of the plateau is included within the work, and the surrounding bluffs are very high and steep. Within No. 9, stone implements, pottery and flint arrow points were very numerous, and the soil rich. If there were entrances or gate-ways, they have been wholly obscured by long cultivation.

Neither here nor in any of the forts on this river, are the lines so constructed as to give mutual support to their several parts. The positions are well chosen for natural strength, but each part of the defense, relied upon its own power of resistance. Here, as usual, there are convenient springs, a rivulet, and the river itself, for supplying water.

Fort No. 11—Plate VII.

The east branch of Rocky river, at Weymouth, rushes through a narrow channel, with vertical walls of rock, seldom more than fifty feet wide, which it has excavated for itself, to a depth about equal to its width. It has assumed the figure of a peninsula, in the form of an ox-bow, about four hundred feet long from base to point. The stream is so rapid, that it has an estimated fall of one hundred and twenty-five feet in a mile and a half, furnishing valuable water power, which the inhabitants have turned to good account.

It would, in this region, be difficult to find a position more inaccessible to an assaulting party, than the water sides of this peninsula. About three hundred feet from its point, the ancient engineers made a triple wall of earth, with exterior ditches, as shown on the plate. From the outer wall to the middle one, is forty-two, and from this to the inner one thirty-eight feet. All the ditches are yet (1850) three feet in depth, and the banks two to three feet high, as represented on the profile $a\ b$. If there were entrances or gate-ways on the land front, they are not now visible. Probably the entrance was effected by wooden steps, that could be easily drawn within the work.

Inside the fort is a low mound, m, and near the road, at the edge of the village, a group of six still smaller and lower ones, which contain human bones. This enclosed space was selected by the early white settlers for a cemetery. As the soil is a stiff clay; and but a few feet in depth, resting upon layers of sandstone flags, it has been abandoned as a place of burial. The crevices of the river ledges were, in the pioneer times, infested with yellow rattle-snakes, from whence in spring they spread themselves over the adjacent country. There is no higher land within arrow shot. This must be regarded as a very secure position, both artificially and by nature.

The Domiciles of the Mound Builders.

The archæologists of Europe have discovered three styles of domicile, which were occupied by pre-historic races. In France and England there are remains of "pit dwellings," probably made with wood, the lower parts sunk several feet into the earth. In Switzerland there are still visible, in the waters of shallow lakes, the foundations of habitations set on piles, which were also places of defence.

An earlier and ruder race in Belgium, and Eastern France occupied natural caves; which are no doubt the primitive domiciles of men.

The caves of the United States, also exhibit evidences of oconpation; but the explorations do not yet show, how many races have made use of them. As at present known the relics of red men predominate.

Over a vast field, extending from the Gulf of Mexico to Lake Superior; the indications of a dense ancient population are conclusive, but we have no certain evidences of the character of their habitations. The temporary shelters of the red races of the north, usually made of boughs, poles and bark, disappear in a few years. In the few cases where they construct cabins, they are wholly of wood, or of wood covered with earth. They are without the cellars of the ancient pit dwellers of Salisbury in England.

The Mandans of the Upper Missouri, and the Digger Indians of the Pacific Coast; have in some cases however put earth on their lodges, making a slight excavation beneath them; which faintly shows the site of their villages. We should expect a people like the Mound Builders who had the intelligence, and the industry; to construct so many, and so extensive earth works; over a territory so broad; would have built for themselves comfortable and permanent dwellings, of which the remains would now be visible.

I wish to call attention to this subject by referring to pits, and artificial cavities; which still exist in the vicinity of ancient earth works in Ohio. In those which I have examined the evidence is by no means conclusive, as to their age or their purposes. The style of the earth works, in different parts of the Mound country, is by no means the same. The differences are such, as to indicate at least three races or nations, as already stated; but they may not have occupied their respective territories at the same time.

Ancient Pits or Cachès.

On the farm of Mr. Andrew Hale at the northeast corner of Bath, in Summit county, are the remains of two very remarkable groups of pits. Fifty years since when Mr. Hale commenced clearing away the heavy forest, which then covered this country; they were quite conspicuous, and were covered with trees of the largest size.

The largest group, was near the south line of lot 11, on a small branch running east into the Cuyahoga river, near where it crosses the north and south lines, between Bath and North Hampton. It consisted of an enclosure or bank of earth of an irregular figure, approaching a pentagon; with the corners rounded off. It was situated at the crest of a terrace, but a few feet above the branch; and was about one hundred and twenty feet across. Nothing but a dim outline is now visible, the ground having been plowed many times over. On the north and west sides at a distance of fifty to sixty rods is a high drift ridge, overlooking the valley of the brook. The soil is dry and gravelly. At present it has the appearance of a broad cavity, with a slightly raised rim. When Mr. Hale first saw it, there was a series of cavities like those hereafter described.

About half a mile north-west of this spot, on a part of the drift ridge just referred to, and at a much greater elevation, there was another but smaller group of pits. Here the embankment was only about thirty feet across. It stood on the edge of a dry gravelly terrace, and overlooked towards the north-west; the valley of Hale's brook. This is also obliterated by the plow.

Less than half a mile down the brook on the south bank stands a similar work, represented in Plate VII. This is still covered with growing trees, one of which is an oak, two and a half feet in diameter. Mr. Hale says it is in all respects like the others except the size. The largest diameter of this is sixty feet, the shorter one thirty. A man standing in the deepest pits can with difficulty look over the highest part of the bank, which encloses them. It is two to four feet high, and the pits two to six feet long, somewhat oblong, and irregular. The breadth of the bank is five to sixteen feet, the soil dry and gravelly, forming part of a plain about twenty feet above the creek. An open cut was made by us, at the south-east corner through the bank, and the pits; and no relics, coals or ashes were found. The bottom of the cavities is clean sand and gravel, and somewhat dish shaped.

On the stream above these remains there had evidently been a village or camp. Old hearths of stone, charcoal and ashes; cover a large space on its northern bank. A large Indian trail passed near this old camp, and thence over the hills to the west; along which there were very old hacks or blazes, upon the trees. In one of them, Mr. H. found a leaden bullet forty years since; which then had sixty annual layers of growth over it. Over one of the axe marks, there was a growth of one hundred and sixty layers. Near by on the hills, was an old and extensive sugar camp of the Indians.

The only other work of this character in this vicinity, is represented on Plate IV., upper corner at the right. It has the same ear like outline, with a narrow entrance; is situated on the edge of a terrace near water like the others, and has eight oblong pits in the interior. It is eighty-two feet in length, thirty feet broad at the narrowest part, and forty-five at the widest. A part of the timber had been cut away but the stumps remained, and the work was not injured by the hand of man. Outside of this group however, were a large number of pits at C; not quite as deep or as regular as those within, which are also represented. On the east are the remains of a slight bank at B, inclosing a space one hundred and sixty feet long by one hundred feet broad; which is in an old field. Mr. George McKisson on whose land it is found, says that in a state of nature, the pits within this embankment, were like those on the other side of the enclosure, at C. Here the soil is dry and gravelly requiring no draining. Some of the pits at C are partly down the side of the bluff; which led me to regard them as remains of cave dwellings, but on cleaning out some of them, and especially after making an open cut across B, it appeared necessary to abandon this conjecture. In one of them was nearly half a cart load of the blue hard pan or clay, which lies twelve to fifteen feet below the surface, and which crops out on the side of the gullies. Numerous springs of water issue at the top of this blue impervious clay.

There is no rim of earth around the edges of these, or of any of the pits. The earth from the enclosed ones at B, is about equal to that of the embankment. It is the same for the one on Plate VII. The earth taken from those which are outside the enclosures, must have been carried away. They appear to have been sunk from two to four feet, with perpendicular sides; probably sustained with wood, and the whole covered with wood or bark, of which nothing remains.

Such cavities are found in many other places in Ohio and the north-west, generally near the old earth works. They are quite numerous on Kelly's Island, opposite Sandusky; where they are regarded as the old cachès of the red man. There is a group of them on the land of Mr. Edmund Ward, partly demolished by the east and west road past his house, which is almost identical with those on the Cuyahoga. In the vicinity implements of polished stone are abundant; such as axes or mauls, chisels, fleshers, and arrow points of flint. There are also on the Island small mounds and enclosures of earth, but as yet no implements of copper have been found there; or any of stone, that may not be of recent Indian make. No certain traces of the Mound Builders are known on this Island.

Around some of the ancient works in the south part of Ohio, there are old pits of irregular form, without borders. They are generally made in dry gravelly soil, and are both within and without the embankments. I have long regarded some of them as the remains of domiciles. If they are not, we have nothing which indicates what shelters were in use, by those old inhabitants.

On the river bluff, above Piketon, in Pike county, there is one which was, in 1839, thirty feet across and twelve feet deep; its outline being a perfect circle. This cavity is precisely what would result from a circular pit, twenty feet across, with upright sides, and about fifteen feet deep. It has not, to my knowledge, been cleared out. If it is an ancient habitation, there must be at the bottom, charcoal and domestic implements of stone.

According to Squier and Davis, at Dunlop's earth work, in Ross county, there are *five*; at another in Liberty township, same county, *twenty*, partly within and partly without the walls; and at "Mound City" there are *twenty* mounds and *seven* pits.

The works represented in Plates XVI and XVII, of the same book; show respectively five and six, large exterior pits. In the southern part of the State there are frequently, large and irregular depressions that hold water, from which part of the earth of the banks was no doubt taken; but most of them are too small in comparison with the embankments, to furnish a material part of the earth for them. They are not as regular or circular as those on the Cuyahoga.

In article 155 of the Smithsonian Contributions (1852), I have described a remarkable series of ancient pits, on the north shore of Portage Lake, in Houghton county, Michigan. These have raised rims or banks, and are large and deep; but are not circular. They have not been opened in such a manner, as to decide for what purpose they were made; and are now in part covered by the village of Hancock. There are in these works features, which indicate more of the domicile than the cachè.

In Montcalm county, Michigan, there is a collection of pits, described by Mr. Steele, which he regards as Indian cachès. Near them are old corn hills. on which are growing pine trees of the usual size for that region. They are two and three feet deep, and there are pine trees in them, the same as those among the ancient hills of corn. There are also relics of the red man in the vicinity.

Mr. Alf D. Jones, of Omaha, has described the earth covered lodges of the Omahas, or Eromahas of the plains. They are twenty feet in diameter and ten feet high, with a long low entrance, like the snow-house of the Eskimos. The weight is sustained by posts and rafters, covered with brush. Over this they lay earth, which is taken in part from within; and in part from an exterior trench. The sites of these abandoned villages, are plainly visible; long after the woody parts of their lodges have disappeared, but the remains are in the form of low mounds, and not of depressions. There are other northern tribes who cover the base of their skin or bark lodges, with earth. Where earth is thrown up around the base of a wigwam, it leaves a low rim or bank generally in the form of a circle.

Major Kennon, of the Russian Telegraph Exploring Company, states that the permanent Kowaks of Siberia, have their lodges partly sunk into the soil. They enter their lodges, through the smoke hole in the top. Such domiciles, when abandoned, would leave circular pits, provided they are sunk so deep, that the earth covering is not sufficient to fill the cavity. At the bottom there is always a pile of ashes and charcoal, mingled with bones and broken utensils. These relics would remain immensely long periods of time; and if our old pits were ever put to the same use, we should find the same evidence of it.

Near Salisbury, in England, there are old pits, usually circular, in all of which remains of fires and of stone implements, are found. I expect that farther examinations in our ancient pits, will show that some of them were sunk as a part of a lodge; but in all that I have opened this evidence is wanting.

Isolated Mounds.

The largest artificial mound of the Cuyahoga Valley, is on the land and near the residence of Col. John Schoonova, in North Hampton. It is now eighteen feet high, and its base is three hundred feet in circumference. Except for the purpose of making a milk house, it has not been opened. A short distance west of it, on a gravel ridge, which corresponds to the second terrace of the valley, is an Indian burial ground; and some irregular cavities, probably cachès. Excavations among the group of mounds, at the corners of Bath, Boston, Richfield and North Hampton townships, have disclosed very little of interest. The contents of one further down the river, in Boston, and of a small work in the same vicinity, have already been noticed. There must have been a time, when this neighborhood was very populous.

Most of the mounds in and near the city of Cleveland have been destroyed. About the year 1820, one which stood on the lot of the Methodist Church, at the corner of Euclid and Erie streets, was partially opened by Dr. T. Garlick and his brother Abel. Two implements were found, one of which was a bodkin or piercing instrument, made of green siliceous slate, very hard, and well polished; its upper or dull end is flattened, to make it more effectual in boring. The other was a piece of the same material, about six and one-half inches long, three wide, and at the middle three-eighths of an inch thick, made thinner towards the ends. Flatwise near the middle, an inch and one-half apart, were two holes, about the size of a rye straw; which tapered towards the center both ways.

This class of stones is very common in Ohio. They are presumed to have been used in sizing, and perhaps in twisting their coarse thread. The size of the holes is quite uniform, and the circular marks of a boring tool are plain. From the mound on Sawtell avenue, opposite the Water Cure, Mr. Goodman and myself took an artificially wrought sphere, made of the iron stone of the coal series, two inches in diameter. It was perforated to the center by two tapering holes, at right angles to each other, by which it was probably suspended, as an ornament. Near it, and about three feet below the top, were four small copper rings or beads. Several feet away, and a little deeper, a stone whistle or call was found, which is figured on Plate VIII. Such whistles, flutes or calls, as they are variously named; are common in the Ohio mounds. Some of them are flattened at the upper end like a bark whistle, and some have holes at the side like a flute. In this the bore is perfectly circular and straight, but tapers slightly towards the mouth hole. The material is fire clay rock of the coal series, polished without and within; the spiral marks of a revolving boring tool, being yet visible.

As this mound forms one of the ornaments of his grounds, Mr. Freese did not wish to have it demolished. Only a small part of it was opened, consisting of a cut from the east side to the center, where it was enlarged several feet in a circular form. At the base was a large bed of rammed gravel and clay, which was followed two and one-half feet below the natural surface; without reaching undisturbed earth. The human skeleton, which almost every mound contains, was not found. To make such examinations complete, the tumulus must be entirely shoveled over, and also all puddled layers that may be noticed beneath it.

The mounds of the lake country, are like the other earth works; much smaller than those on the waters of the Ohio, but there is a close resemblance in the relics, throughout both regions. Their weapons of war are so imperfectly known, that they can neither be said to have been similar or dissimilar.

There is no evidence that either of these ancient nations, made general war upon each other. Their fortified camps and villages, were more likely intended for the security of clans and tribes of the same people, against each other; like the feudal castles with which Europe is thickly dotted over.

Among the works of the lake folk, are none which have a religious aspect. There are no "altar mounds," truncated pyramids, or raised platforms; such as are common farther south.

Our aborigines have been seen to erect mounds of stone over their dead, and very rarely mounds of earth. But in all cases theirs are small and low, and the bodies were not burned. There is little difficulty in distinguishing the Indian, from the Mound Builder tumulus, by its external aspects, but if there are doubts on this point, they are always put to rest when the relics are exhumed.

Rock Inscriptions.

As yet it is not known of what substance, or in what form the ancient inhabitants fashioned their picks. It is evident they must have had an instrument for this purpose, not only hard enough to work up earth, clay and hard pan; but to cut sand stone, lime rock, and granite boulders.

The rock inscriptions at Independence, Plate IX, were made upon a very hard surface of grindstone grit, in which the marks of a sharp pick, are too plain to be mistaken. Those described by Mr. Squier, on the Guyandotte river, in West Virginia, are worked out in the same way. On a flat grit of the coal series, a mile above Wellsville, on the north shore of the Ohio, is a large group of uncouth effigies, sunk into the rock by means of a pick. These are the work of the Indians. Those figured by Mr. Jas. W. Ward on boulders of sandstone, near Barnesville, Belmont Co., O., are in a less hard material, and the points of the tool are not as plain, but are visible.

There is reason to believe that the Independence and the Belmont County inscriptions, are more ancient than the others, and perhaps they are of the age of the Mound Builders.

This people certainly wrought the copper mines of Point Kewenaw, on Lake Superior. On the walls of copper veins worked by them, I have seen marks of a pick; but no copper tool has been found, or at least not described; which would answer this purpose.

During the bronze period in Europe, people had such a tool made of metal; and those made of horn, bone or wood were common in the stone period.

The Winnebagoes who mined lead at Dubuque, in Iowa; nearly a century since, had a pick made of the horn of a deer, with a handle of wood. This evidently would not cut away the grits of Ohio, or the trap and granite boulders, on which we see the marks of a sharp and hard point. It might have been done by a point of flint or quartz, inserted in a stock of horn or bone; but as yet no such points have been described.

The ancients also needed something resembling a pick, to work the flint quarries, of which there are many in Ohio. In working up ordinary earth, hoes, spades and picks of bone, could easily be made; but none of them have been found in the mounds. Spades, and probably hoes, of native copper have been found.

The Independence Stone.

Great care has been taken to obtain a correct sketch, of what remains of this inscription. A very rude drawing of it was published in Schoolcraft's great work upon the Indian tribes, in 1854. He probably regarded it as the work of the red man. In 1869, Dr. J. H. Salisbury, of this city, who has long been engaged in the investigation of rock inscriptions at the West, in company with Dr. Lewis, of the Asylum at Newburg, made a copy by means of full and exact measurements.

As no sketch is of equal authenticity with a photograph, Mr. Thos. T. Sweeny, an artist of Cleveland, at our request went to Independence, and took a copy with his instrument. The light on that day was not favorable, but the outlines of all the artificial work upon the stone, were thus secured with exactness. For the purposes of the engraver, the figures were filled in by Dr. Salisbury from his sketch. The engravers, Messrs. Morgan & Vallendar, have made of this perfected copy a faithful transcript.

Without expressing an opinion as to the authors of these inscriptions, I present, in connection with the engraving, the details furnished by Dr. Salisbury:

"Description of Sculptured Rocks at Independence, Cuyahoga Co., O.

"By J. H. Salisbury, M. D.

"*History.*—Mr. W. F. Bushnell, who resides at Independence, and M. B. Wood, of Cleveland, state that these markings were discovered about 1853, while stripping the earth from the surface of a quarry, on the north brow of the hill on which the village of Independence stands. Here the rocks projected in the form of a perpendicular cliff, from twenty to forty feet in height. On the top of this cliff, and near its edge, the markings were discovered. The soil over the markings was from five to eight inches in depth, and was black, having been formed from decaying vegetation. A tree was growing directly over the markings, that was one foot or more in diameter. Within a few feet of the spot there was an oak tree, over four feet in diameter. This tree—some years previous to the discovery of the sculptured rock—had fallen nearly across the markings, and in 1853 was much decayed. Besides the markings represented in Plate IX, there were others adjacent, belonging to the same group; which had been destroyed by the quarry men, before Messrs. Bushnell and Wood were aware of it. Among the markings destroyed were the outline figures of a male and female, very well executed. There were also the representations of the wolf's foot, and figures of the feet of other animals.

"At the time of the discovery the stone church at Independence was being built; and, at the suggestion of Deacon Bushnell and others, all the markings not previously destroyed, were carefully cut out and the block placed in the rear wall of the church, about eight feet above the ground. It was prudently placed at this height to prevent its being defaced.

"In company with Dr. Lewis, Superintendent of the Northern Ohio Lunatic Asylum, I visited the locality on the 5th day of June, 1869, and made careful drawings of all the markings visible on the block, in the rear wall of the church. These with accurate measurements, are represented in Plate IX, made more perfect by the use of Mr. Sweeney's photography.

"*Description.*—The rock here described only contains a portion of the inscription. The balance was destroyed in quarrying. The markings on the portion of the rock preserved, consist of the human foot clothed with something like a moccasin or stocking; of the naked foot; of the open hand; of round markings, one in front of the great toe of each representation of the clothed foot; the figure of a serpent; and a peculiar character *w*, which might be taken for a rude representation of a crab or crawfish, but which bears a closer resemblance to an old-fashioned spear head, used in capturing fish.

"The clothed feet are of five different sizes. There are eighteen impressions of this kind, arranged in nine pairs. Of the largest size, there are five pairs, *a, c, g, l, m*. Of the next size smaller, there is only one pair, *o*. Of the next smaller size, one pair, *q*. Of the next smaller size, one pair, *e*; and of the smallest size, one pair. Of the naked foot there is only a single figure, which is rudely carved, and which is much longer than the clothed representations. There are two figures of the open hand—one with a large palm and short fingers—the other smaller, with the fingers long and slender.

"The sculptures have all been made with a sharp pointed instrument, by the process of *pecking*, and sunk in throughout, instead of being mere outlines. The cuttings are from one-eighth to half an inch deep. The two hands are sculptured the deepest. In the illustrations, I have endeavored to give an idea of the markings left by the tool used; though these are less evident than the representations.

"The length of the largest feet in figures *a, c, g, l, m*, from the extremity of the great toe to the heel is six and three-fourths inches, and the width at the widest place two and three-fourths inches. The length of the next in size *o*, is five inches and width two and one-eighth inches, and of *q* five inches by two inches Length of next smaller size *e*, three and a half inches and width one and three-fourth inches, and three and three-fourth inches by one and a half inches. The length of the naked foot *s*, is nine inches, and greatest width four and three-fourths inches. The great toe is one inch long, the second toe one and one-fourth inches long,— the third toe one and a half inches long; the fourth toe one and a fourth inches in length, and the little toe one inch long.

"In the large hand *t*, the palm is five and a half inches long and three and a half inches wide. The length of the thumb is one and a half inches,— the index finger one and three-fourths inches,— the middle finger two inches,— the ring finger one and three-fourths inches, and the little finger one and a half inches. In the other hand *u*,— the palm is three and a half inches long and two and a half inches wide. The length of the thumb is two and one-fourth inches,— the index finger two and a half inches;— the middle finger two and three-fourths inches; the ring finger two and one-fourth inches; and the little finger two inches.

The diameter of the circular markings,— invariably found in front of the clothed feet, are as follows :— *b*, one and one-eighth inches; *d*, one and three-fourths inches; *f*, three-fourths inch; *h*, one inch; *k*, half inch; *n*, one and a half inches; *p*, one and one-fourth inches; *p*, one inch.

" The diameter of the serpent's head is two and three-fourths inches. Length of body ninety-four inches,— making the entire length of the figure about eight feet.

" In the sculptured figure *w*, the measurements are omitted.

" It is evident this slab does not contain the entire inscription. The tracks *l*, are only partially present; while it is very probable that more tracks occurred in the direction *a b*, arranged in a line as those are from *c* to *l*, where there are ten tracks and eight round characters, and which are probably not all that were orginally in this line, previous to the stones being quarried. The round markings in front of the clothed tracks, may have been intended to represent the tracks of dogs or cats; but at present they are so smoothed by time, that it is impossible to make out anything but simple irregular circular depressions.

" The rock on which the inscription occurs, is the grindstone grit of the Ohio Reports, an extensive stratum in Northern Ohio, about one hundred and fifty feet below the conglomerate. It is almost pure silex, and possesses the property of resisting atmospheric changes to a remarkable degree. Boulders and projecting portions of the formation, from which this block was obtained,— that have been exposed to the weather for ages,— preserve perfectly their sharp angular projections. As a building stone, it is superior, on account of its extreme durability. This durability of the rock, and the fact that these markings were covered with earth, explains why they have been so finely preserved.

" The markings *a, c, e, g, l, m, o* and *q*, have been supposed by some to represent the tracks of the buffalo. After carefully measuring and drawing them, however, I have come to the conclusion that they were designed to represent tracks of the clothed human foot, and as such have described them.

"The so called bird tracks which are few and faint on this slab, are numerous and bold on most of the rock inscriptions of Ohio."

Serpent Effigies.

The serpent or snake in some of its varieties, has had much to do with the symbolic worship of nations, especially the rude and ancient nations. This is shown not only in history, and as far back as we get information from this source; but from inscriptions and effigies, that extend to still more ancient periods.

In the third chapter of Genesis it is referred to as an example of subtlety, and is made the representative of evil or satanic power. By the oriental nations it is regarded as the embodiment of sagacity and cunning, allied to wisdom. Our Saviour desired his disciples to be as "wise as serpents," which in their circumstances inculcated a high form of prudence.

Dr. Kalisch an eminent student of the Asiatic people, says it is generally represented as the emblem of evil, disobedience, and contumely; but the Phœnicians and Chinese use it as a symbol of wisdom and power. The last named people imagine that the kings of heaven, have the bodies of serpents. It appears with great frequency among their pictorial representations.

In Egypt this reptile was worshiped, as a symbol of health and life. It was probably in this aspect, that the Children of Israel regarded the brazen serpent, set up by Moses.

The early inhabitants of our continent, placed the snake foremost among their sculptures and their effigies. Among the North American Indians the evil principle is worshiped, or if not adored, is the object of supplication, as much as the good. The Ojibwas have their good and their bad Manitous, to both of whom they offer sacrifice and prayer. As a living creature they respect the snake, and treat it kindly. In ancient Mexico it was an object of worship.

It is not therefore strange, that we find among the earth mounds of Ohio and Wisconsin; some which are in the form of a serpent. It was here as in Asia and probably in all parts of the world, an animal which symbolized something, which was held sacred. The sculptured effigies at Independence in this county and near Barnesville in Belmont county, O., with their surroundings, are no doubt records of religious sentiments or formulas, the meaning of which remains a mystery.

Those made upon the sand rock near Wellsville, on the Ohio, are evidently the work of the red man, and among many animals and human beings grotesquely cut, is a rude rattlesnake with a fancy head.

Serpent worship being as it were inherent with the barbarous and semi-barbarous races in all countries, there is nothing marvelous in finding evidences of it here.

Spindle Socket Stones.

On Plate No. VIII is a Photographic copy, of one of hundreds of stones; found in this valley and throughout Northern Ohio. On one side, and sometimes on both, are circular cup-shaped cavities, from a mere point to a diameter of an inch and a half. They are nearly half the diameter in depth, and are perfectly symmetrical, forming nearly a hemisphere a little flattened. I have seen none that exceed an inch and a half across, and none that are deeper than the semi-diameter. They are evidently formed by revolution, for they are smooth and the section is a true circle. They are so numerous that they must have been in general use for domestic purposes. I have never seen them described among the relics of the mounds, or the implements of the savage races now in existence.

From accounts that have reached us, of the mode of spinning among the Aztecs, and also the modern Mexicans; they used an upright wooden spindle like the stem of a top, on which was a stone collar to act as a balance wheel. The Romans, Greeks and Egyptians had something similar to this. The Puebla Indians have been seen spinning cotton, on such a spindle fifteen and eighteen inches long, the foot of which rested in a bowl. None of the descriptions are very minute, as to the mode of twirling this primitive spindle. It could be done by hand, or by a cord, wound several times around it, and pulled back and forth; or by a bow-string, worked each way, as the Iroquois did when they got fire by friction. The most primitive way of making twine is by twisting it between the thumb and forefinger, which is nearly as rapid as with a spindle worked by hand; but with a spindle the thread can be wound, as fast as it is made, into a bunch by reversing the motion.

In France and Italy there are peasants, who made thread recently on a wooden spindle with a stone whorl, or balance, twirled by hand; and in the island of Islay, an old woman was seen spinning with a stick, on which she had impaled a potatoe to give it a steadier motion.

It was not till the eighteenth century, that spindles were propelled by wheels, which did not change the principle; but only increased the speed and steadiness.

We know the Mound Builders had a very coarse fabric like hemp, the threads of which resembled in size those of the gunny bags, made by an equally rude people in India. They may have cultivated some plant for its fiber, or they may have appropriated that of the nettle, as the first settlers of the Miami valley did, who found it very durable.

If a small socket was made in a stone, or a piece of wood for the foot of a spindle, which also passed through a hole or a forked stick, to steady it above; a very rapid motion could be got up, by the bow-string; and the process of spinning carried on by one person. The foot of the spindle would wear a smooth round cavity, precisely such as we see on these stones. When it became deep the friction would increase, and its foot would be changed to another place on the same stone. Some of them are so near each other, that the rim between them is cut away.

In the Ohio mounds, and on the surface, there is found flat circular stones, with a hole in the center, such as are found in England, and in the Swiss lake dwellings, where they are called " spindle whorls."

There is found also among the remains of the pile dwellings of the European lakes, a coarse cloth made of flax.

These facts induce me to regard these cavities, as part of the spinning apparatus of the fort builders. The northern Indians were dressed in skins, when they were first encountered by the whites, and did not know the use of cloth. Their nets were made of coarse twine from the prepared bark of trees, and their mats from flat strips of bark or of rushes.

In lower latitudes, on the waters of the Gulf of Mexico and California, the Indians had cloth made of cotton, as they make it now.

The stone represented here is one of six specimens in the museum of the Western Reserve Historical Society.

THUMB AND FINGER STONES.

There is in our collection a large representation of water worn pebbles and other stones, which have on each side an artificial cavity, which is not as large, as deep, or smooth; as the spindle socket. These stones are generally elongated and flattened pebbles, not trimmed or altered except as to the artificial depression, or thumb place. Many of them are not of hard material, and the sunken places are often rough, as though they were sunk with a pick, not bored out by a revolving tool. The size of the depressions is about that of the end of a thumb, and they are exactly opposite each other. Some of them would not weigh more than a quarter of a pound, rising to a weight of two pounds. They are found on the surface and in the mounds. We have one which a party from our society took, from a depth of three feet below the natural surface, beneath a mound five feet in height, in North Hampton, Summit county, Ohio, about a year since. It lay among the remains of a charred skeleton, and with it were two flint arrow points, one of which is figured in Plate VIII.

Most of those I have examined have their ends bruised and fractured, as though they were used as a light hammer. Mr. Wilson, in his work on the ancient stone implements of Scandinavia, refers to hammers which he considers were flint breakers. Mr Evans describes similar stones, and both of these authors made flints with pebbles, used as hammers. With those in our collection, even where the pebble is soft, I can easily chip fragments of the hornstones or flint, from the Ohio pits.

Savage nations the world over have modes of manufacturing flint implements. After the block or piece is rudely trimmed by blows from a stone maul, flakes are split off by quick strokes with a small stone hammer. These splinters are fashioned by light blows of bone or horn chisels, or by a slight of hand pressure with a wooden implement; throwing off light flakes. Obsidian quartz and glassy lava are wrought in the same way.

Ancient Flint Quarries.

Arrow points of flint or chert are so common in Ohio, that the sources of supply must have been large. Among the strata of our coal series are numerous bands of limestone, that frequently pass into chert, hornstone and flint. The famous "buhrstone," in Jackson and Vinton counties, is one of those strata; which, like all others of the coal-bearing rocks of Ohio, are very irregular in thickness, quality and extent.

It has long been known that a flint bed existed in Licking county, near Newark; and that it had been extensively quarried in ancient times. The old pits are now visible, covering more than a hundred acres. They are partially filled with water, and are surrounded by piles of broken and rejected fragments; for it is only clear homogenous pieces, that can be wrought into arrow and spear points. With what tools and appliances the ancients wrought such extensive quarries, has not yet been settled. This flint is of a grayish white color, with cavities of brilliant quartz crystals. It appears the stones were sorted, and partially chipped into shape, on the ground; after which they were carried great distances over the country as an article of traffic; arrow points from these quarries having been found in Michigan. Many acres of ground are now covered with flint chips—the result of this trimming process. The business of manufacturing arrows, knives, spears and scrapers, no doubt became a trade among the Mound Builders, as it is known to have been among the Indians. What tools they used for this work is not known, although I conjecture that this was the use of the thumb stones.

Flint arrow heads and implements, are not plenty among the relics of the mounds; but on the surface they are found on nearly every cultivated farm in Northern Ohio. They were in general use among the red men, when the whites first came into their country.

The Indians must therefore have worked the flint quarries, more extensively than the prior race. Several other places are now known besides "Flint Ridge," where old quarries are visible.

There are some on the land of James Hoile, two miles south of Alliance, in Stark county, near the C. & P. Railroad. Here the color of the flint is red, white and mottled.

Flint beds are also known in Tuscarawas county, west of the Muskingum River.

The color in some localities is black. There are ancient excavations in Coshocton county, two miles south of Warsaw, which were doubtless made to procure the dark colored, impure chert, which here sometimes overlies a bed of cannel coal.

On the Great Kanawha, in West Virginia, above Charleston, is a heavy chert bed, on the outcrop of which probably such quarries will be found.

There is another on the Alleghany river, above Freeport, in Pennsylvania.

It is on and near to rivers capable of canoe navigation, that the flint beds should be most extensively wrought, because the product could be more easily transported.

Every Indian hunter required a large number of arrow points, and scarcely a day would pass, without losing some of them. As the Mound Builders were more of agriculturists, and less of hunters, they would require and would consequently scatter fewer of them over the country. Those which are found so profusely on the surface, must have belonged principally to the red race.

It was easier to fabricate knives, cutting edges, and warlike instruments, to be fastened in wooden handles, than the common arrow point; and yet very few flint implements are found, which were designed for such uses. In other countries, in early times, flint cutters were very abundant. They seem to have been among all people, the first invention to answer the purposes of modern cutlery. The Jews used flint knives upon their sacrifices. They have also been found in the Egyptian pyramids.

As late as the battle of Hastings, the English are supposed to have used flint pointed arrows, against William of Normandy. Several thousand flakes, knives and arrows, have been taken out of the later quaternary or drift deposits, in England and France; of the era of the cave man, made from flint nodules of the chalk.

The Digger Indians of California, who represent the diluvial cave dwellers, in their mental and moral developments; manufacture flint knives and arrows at this time.

In Mexico the lowest order of natives do the same, with obsidian—a volcanic glass thrown out of volcanoes.

A general prevalence of these simple cutting implements, among the relics of a lost people, is quite conclusive proof that they were very near to their primitive condition.

Relics of the Mound Builders

IN THE MUSEUM OF THE SOCIETY, JAN., 1871.

Charred cloth from an ancient mound in Butler county, Ohio; procured by Hon. JOHN WOODS.

Bone beads, and red flint arrow point from a mound in Lawrenceburg, Indiana.

Small earthen kettle, from same mound. A. G. GAGE, Esq.

These may be relics of the red man.

Fac-similes in wood, of two stone implements from an ancient mound, corner of Euclid and Erie streets, Cleveland; taken out by Dr. T. GARLICK, in 1820.

They were made of a fine grained greenish striped metamorphic slate found on Lake Superior. One is a bodkin five inches long; the other a flat thin polished stone, six inches long, three wide, and three-eighths thick in the middle, handsomely thining towards the ends. There are two holes through it at the center, made flatwise, one and a half inches apart, which taper towards the middle. This is a common relic of the mounds, and appears to have been used in spinning the coarse netting or cloth made by that people.

Portion of a human jaw and teeth, three feet below a mound on NATHANIEL POINTS' land, Boston, Summit county, Ohio; also a thumb and finger stone; part of a call or whistle made of clay iron stone, and two flint arrow heads, without necks. (Plate VIII.)

Portion of an Oak Post, forming part of a row around a human skeleton, from a mound of loose stone forty feet high, near Jackstown, Licking county, Ohio. I. N. WILSON. Newark, Ohio.

Plates of silvery Mica, from an ancient work near Portsmouth, O.

A sphere of Iron Ore, two inches in diameter, with holes for suspending it, made at right angles to each other. Four copper beads or rings. A stone call or whistle of fire clay rock. (See Plate VIII.) From a mound on the homestead of A. FREESE, Esq., Sawtell avenue, Cleveland, Ohio.

Fac-simile in wood of a large copper dagger or dirk, wrought from a nugget, found seven feet below the surface at Ontonagon, Lake Superior. A. W. ECKHART.

Numerous other copper tools calculated for cutting wood, for mining, and for weapons, have been found near the mouth of the Ontonagon river, and at the ancient copper mines ten to twelve miles up the river. The Mound Builders worked these mines probably two thousand years or more ago.

SPINDLE SOCKET STONES.

1. Kelly's Island, engraved Plate VIII, from a Photograph of the original. Dr. E. STERLING.

2. Independence, Cuyahoga co., Ohio. W. H. KNAPP.

3. East Cleveland. P. H. BABCOCK.

4. Chattanooga, Tenn. Dr. J. S. NEWBERRY.

5. Northfield, Cuyahoga county, Ohio. A. and L. BLISS.

Fac-simile in copper of a spear head, from an ancient mound near Sterling Illinois. *Chicago Academy of Natural Science.*

Pieces of skids and shovels of wood, and mauls of stone; from the ancient copper mines of Lake Superior, ten to twenty feet below the surface.

Among the numerous relics of the aborigines or red men, are some that probably belong to the Mound Builders, but in separating them we place nothing to the credit of this race, where there is doubt in regard to its origin.

They had some stone implements in common; and they have been left by both races in the same mounds.

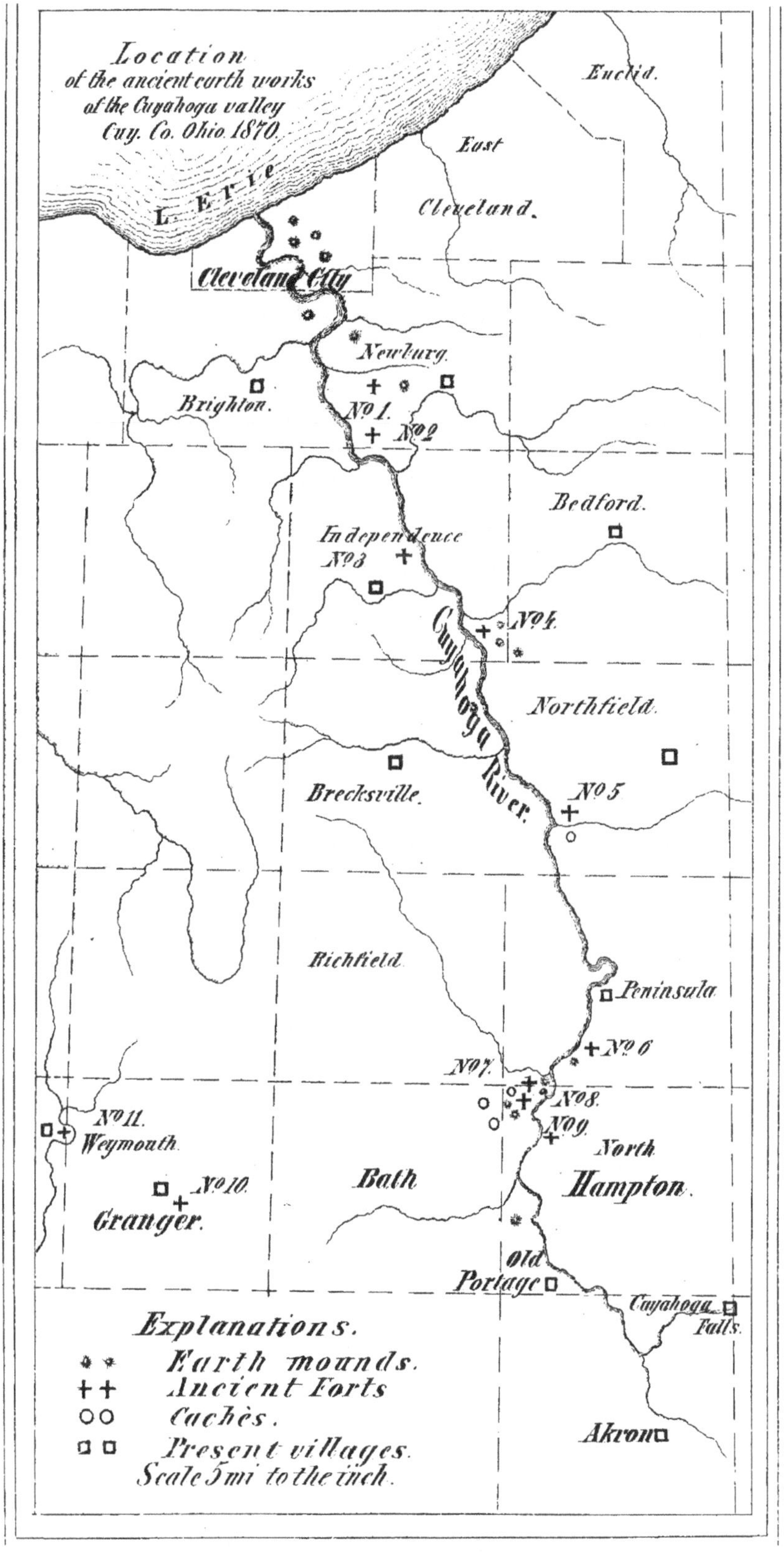

Location
of the ancient earth works
of the Cuyahoga valley
Cuy. Co. Ohio 1870.
L. Erie
Euclid.
East
Cleveland.
Cleveland City
Newburg.
Brighton.
No 1.
No 2
Bedford.
Independence
No 3
No 4.
Cuyahoga River.
Northfield.
Brecksville.
No 5
Richfield.
Peninsula
No 6
No 7.
No 8.
No 9.
No 11.
Weymouth.
North
Hampton.
Bath
No 10.
Granger.
Old
Portage
Cuyahoga
Falls.
Explanations.
Earth mounds.
Ancient Forts
Cachès.
Present villages.
Scale 5 mi to the inch.
Akron

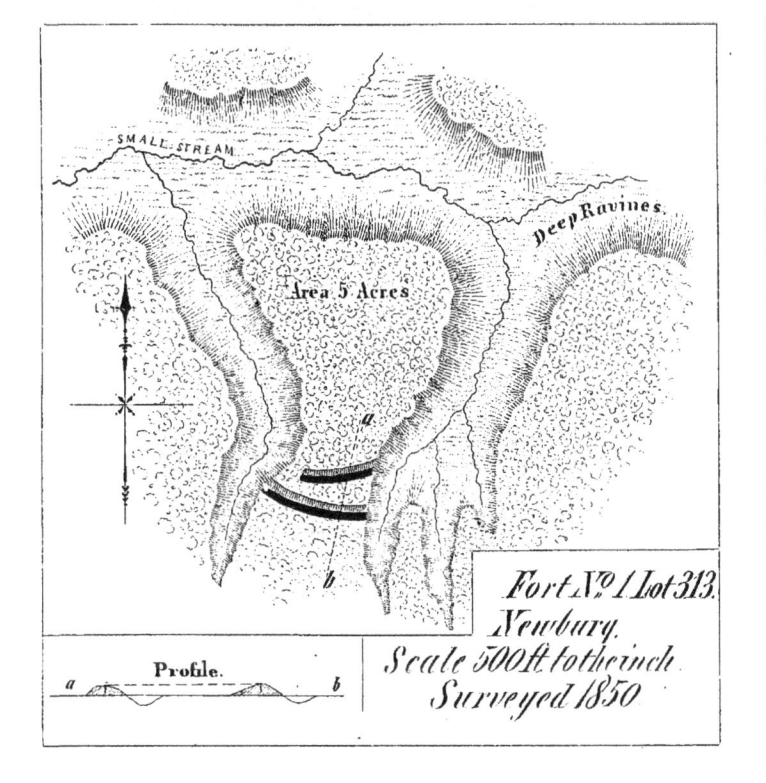

Fort No. 1. Lot 313.
Newbury.
Scale 500 ft to the inch.
Surveyed 1850.

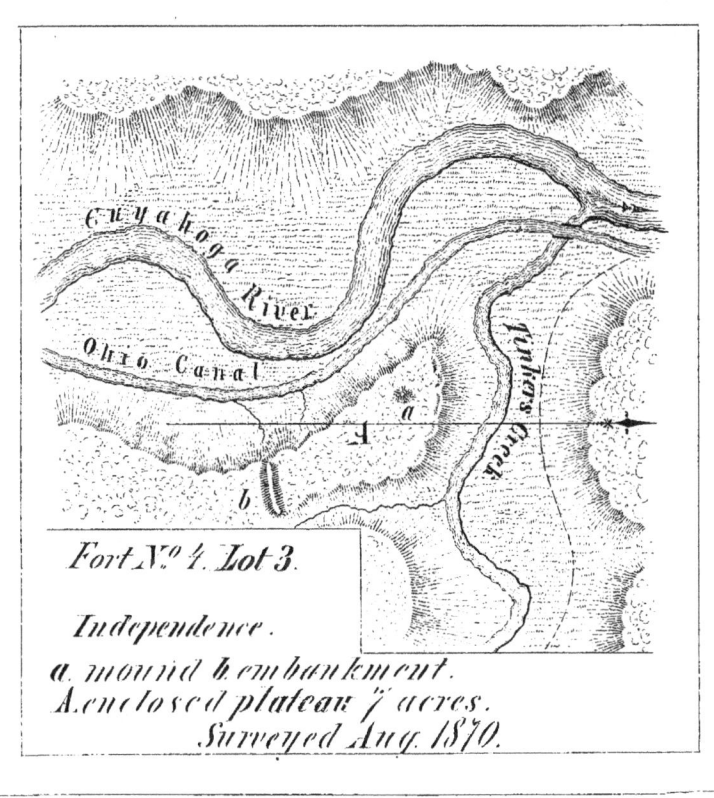

Fort No. 4. Lot 3.
Independence.
a. mound b. embankment.
A. enclosed plateau 7 acres.
Surveyed Aug. 1870.

III.

Fort N° 3. Lot 1. Tract 3.
Independence.
Surveyed 1847 – 1870.

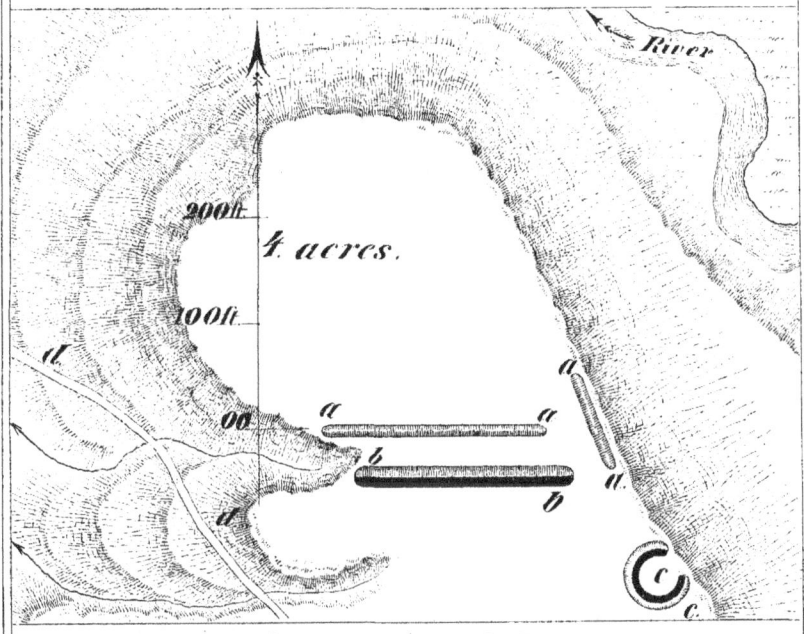

a.a. embankments now obliterated.
b.b. embankment & ditch — c.c. out work.
d.d. road Newburg to Independence.

OUTLINE MAP OF OHIO
Showing the position of the principal Ancient Earth Works.
Ch⁵ Whittlesey. 1864.

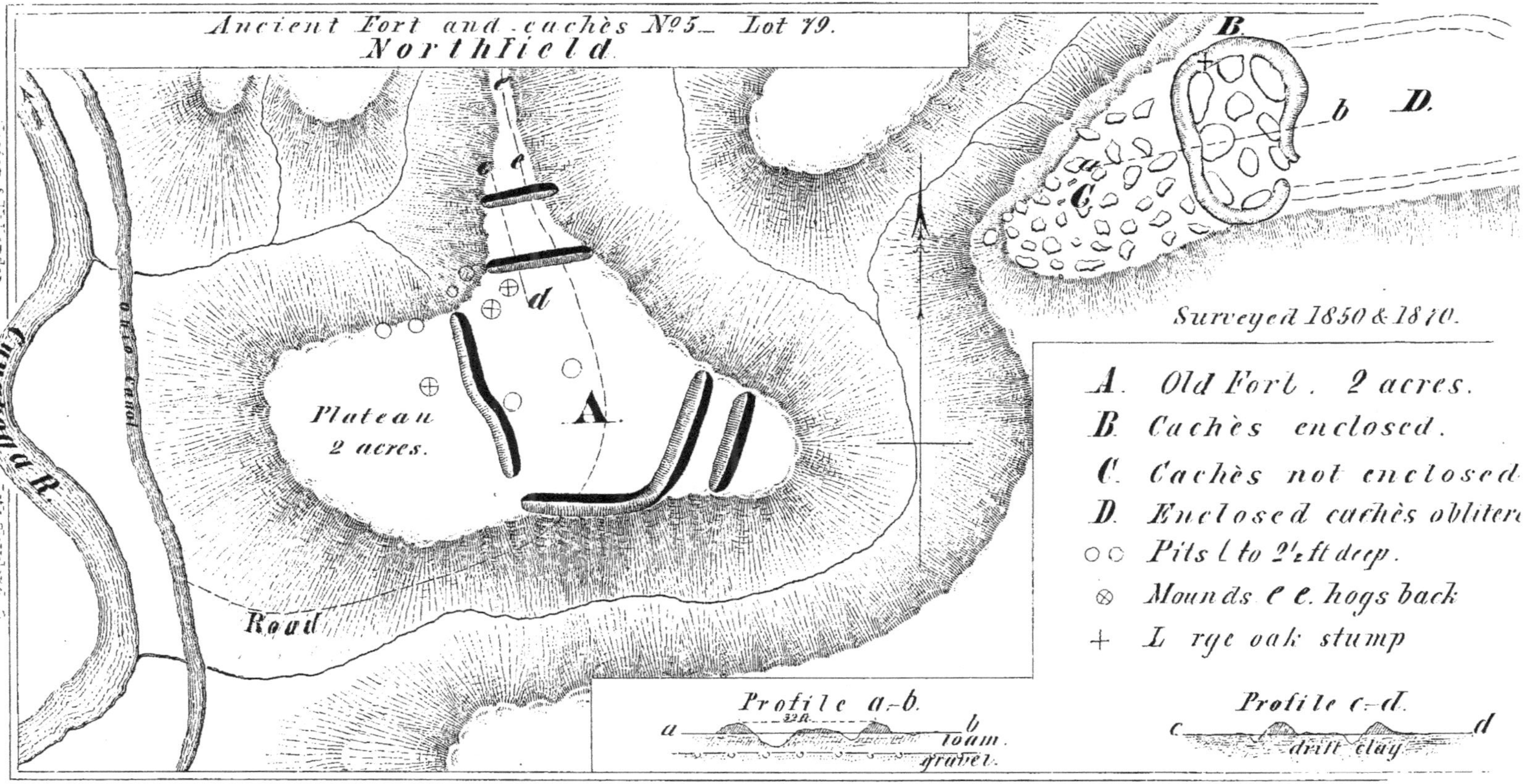
Ancient Fort and caches No. 5 _ Lot 79.
Northfield.
A.
B.
C.
D.
a
b
c
d
e e
Plateau
2 acres.
Road
Ohio Canal
Cuyahoga R.
Surveyed 1850 & 1870.
A. Old Fort. 2 acres.
B. Cachès enclosed.
C. Cachès not enclosed.
D. Enclosed cachès obliter
○ ○ Pits 1 to 2½ ft deep.
⊗ Mounds e e. hogs back
+ Large oak stump
Profile a-b.
32 ft.
loam.
gravel.
Profile c-d.
drift clay.

Fort No 6. BOSTON. Surveyed 1869.

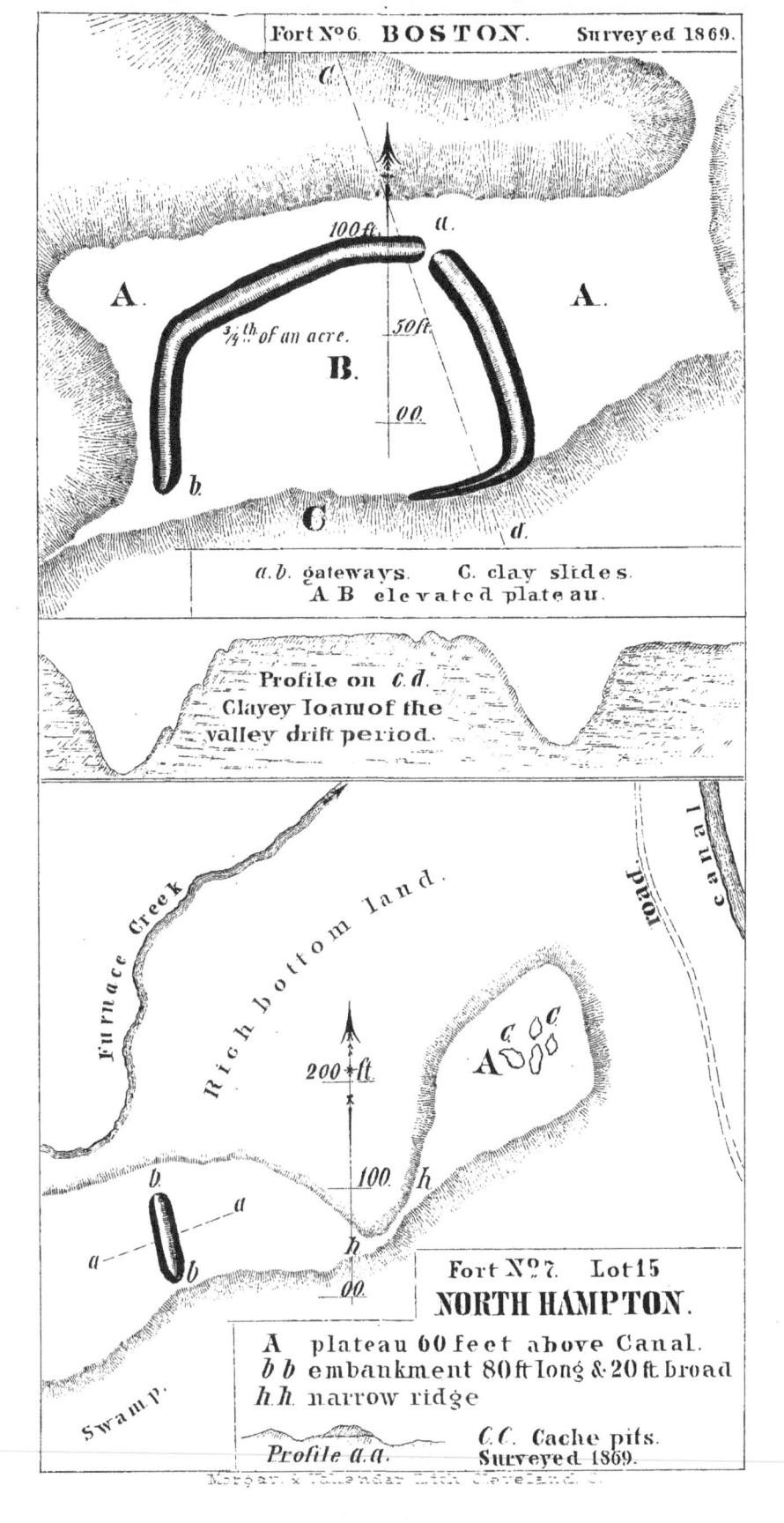

a.b. gateways. C. clay slides.
A B elevated plateau.

Profile on *c.d.*
Clayey loam of the valley drift period.

Fort No 7. Lot 15 NORTH HAMPTON.

A plateau 60 feet above Canal.
b b embankment 80 ft long & 20 ft broad
h.h. narrow ridge
C.C. Cache pits.
Profile *a.a.*
Surveyed 1869.

NORTH HAMPTON. 1870.

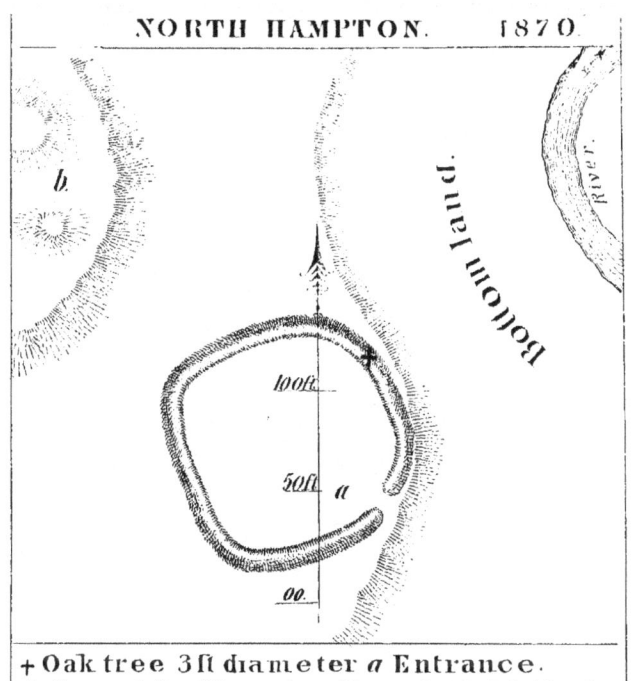

+ Oak tree 3 ft diameter *a* Entrance.
b Gravel knolls of valley drift 50 ft. high

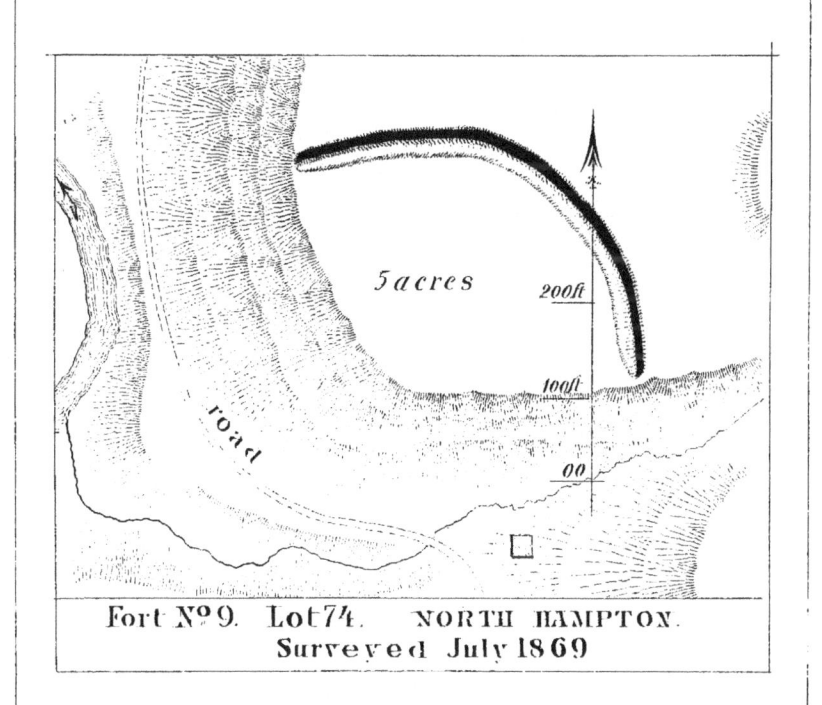

Fort Nº 9.   Lot 74.   NORTH HAMPTON.
Surveyed July 1869

Enclosed caches. Lot. 13
N HAMPTON O 1870

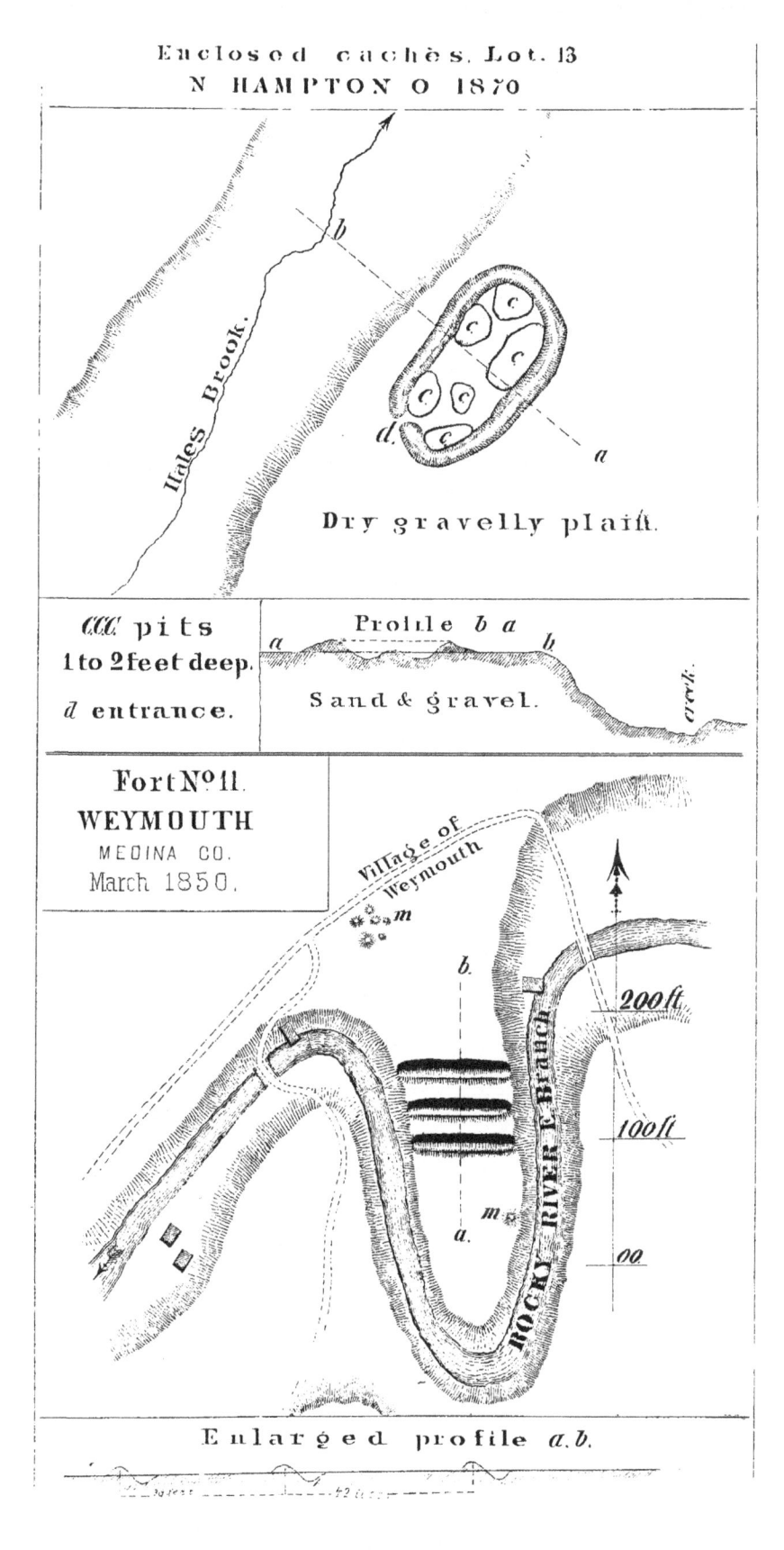

Hales Brook.

Dry gravelly plain.

ccc pits
1 to 2 feet deep.
d entrance.

Profile *b a*

Sand & gravel.

creek.

Fort Nº 11.
WEYMOUTH
MEDINA CO.
March 1850.

Village of Weymouth

ROCKY RIVER E. Branch

200 ft
100 ft
00

Enlarged profile *a.b.*

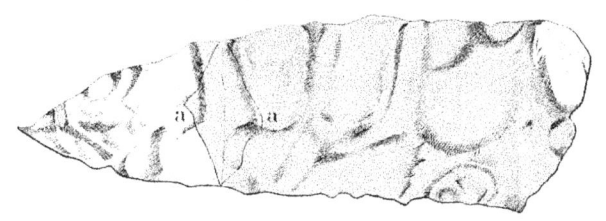

Outline of an **ARROW POINT** of whitish gray
flint from an ancient grave beneath a mound
North Hampton, Summit Co. Ohio.,
a a cross Section. Size of nature

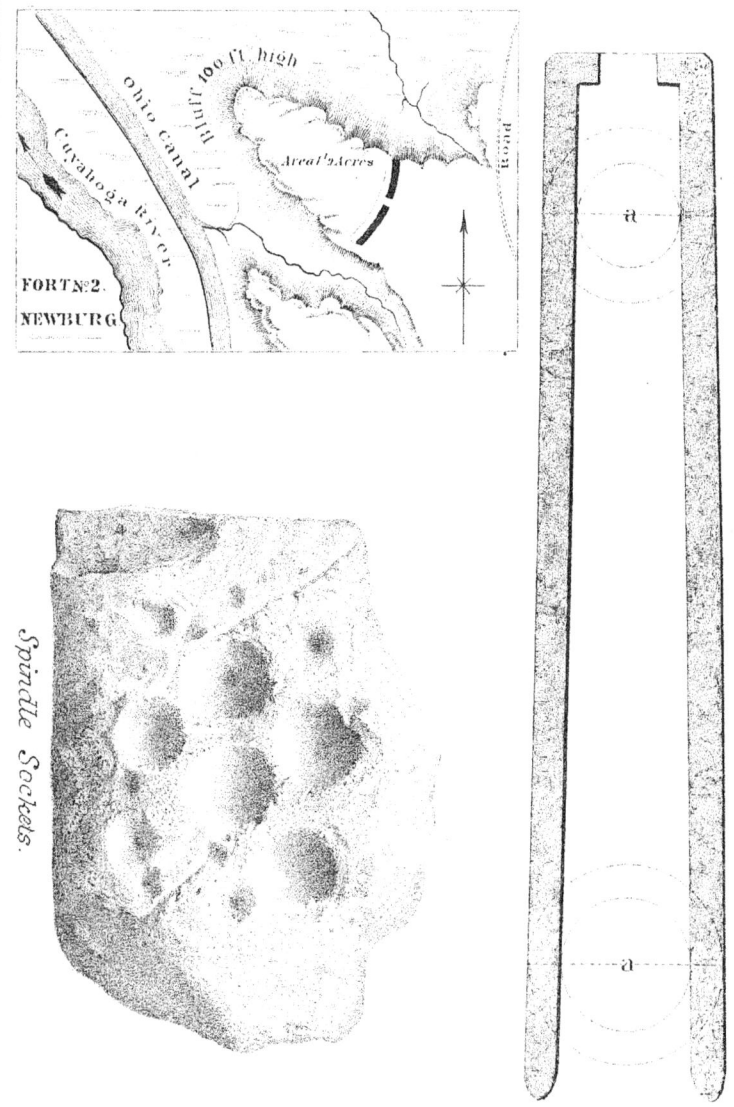

Spindle Sockets.

Section of a Stone Whistle from
a mound on Sawtell Avenue
Cleveland Fire clay rock
Size of nature a a cross section

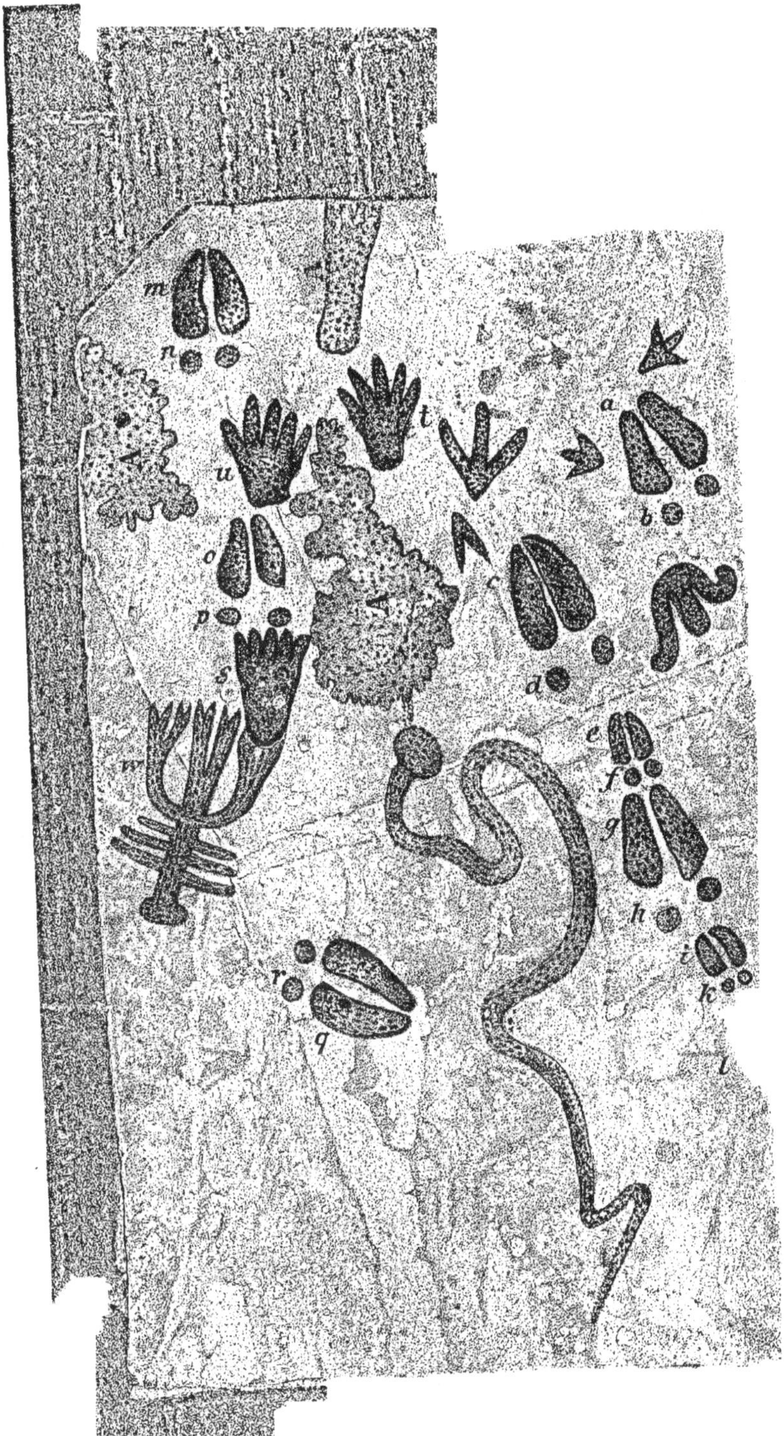
m
n
u
t
a
b
o
c
p
d
s
e
f
g
w
h
i
k
r
q
l

WESTERN RESERVE AND NORTHERN OHIO

istorical Society

AND MUSEUM

THIRD FLOOR OF SAVINGS BANK, ON THE PARK,

CLEVELAND, O.

OFFICERS OF THE SOCIETY, 1870-71.

CHAS. WHITTLESEY, PRESIDENT.

M. B. SCOTT,
J. H. SALISBURY, } VICE PRESIDENTS.

A. T. GOODMAN, SECRETARY.

SAMUEL WILLIAMSON, TREASURER.

CURATORS.

JOSEPH PERKINS,	C. T. SHERMAN,	C. C. BALDWIN,
H. M. CHAPIN,	JOHN W. ALLEN,	WM. BINGHAM,
H. A HARVEY,	B. A. STANARD,	JAMES BARNETT.

Made in the USA
Middletown, DE
24 July 2023